# A Piece of Me Brings Peace To Me

An Autobiographical Collection

*Part 1: The Introduction*

By
Ash'iz "Tha Rebirth"

Copyright © 2017 by Ash'iz Tha Rebirth / Ashley Cuffee

All rights reserved.

ISBN 978-1-62806-126-0

Library of Congress Control Number 2017937026

Published by Salt Water Media, LLC
29 Broad Street, Suite 104
Berlin, MD 21811
www.saltwatermedia.com

The cover image is used courtesy of unsplash.com via the Creative Commons Zero license with special credit to Gaelle Marcel. See unsplash.com for more details.

# Dedication

Here's to the broken... the misunderstood... to the believer of more than your eyes can see... the hope-filled dreamer. Here's to the pieces of us all that when fit together portray the beauty of our authentic destiny and purpose!

# Foreword

We met Ashley on an ordinary day at the park. We knew instantly she was extraordinary.

She is like the ancient water diviners combing the parched and thirsty land for wells. Words drop into her from above. She holds them lovingly. She is a word diviner in a world that needs them.

She channels rhythm and beat, blending sound with stories of light and dark. We breath with her, we feel with her and we are transformed with her. Our souls nourished.

She has poetry in her veins. It is her very lifeblood. Her very essence. Her purpose. She is made of stardust, like all of us. Her beauty rises from the ashes of when she was reborn.

*Written with love by*
*Sophie Burbage & Cynthia Burbage*
*February 26, 2017*

# Preface

I give of myself; sacrifice my truths for the restoring of hope in hearts, the renewing of truth in minds and the understanding of freedom in the spirit! As you indulge in the pouring out of my journey's testament, my prayer and belief is that your journey's testament will be given fresh wind that will encompass your being and begin to manifest it's true meaning, giving you the needed understanding and ability to embrace life as it's been given.

## Dear You

Dear You,
I'm daily preparing for our acquaintance
To prepare my mind for what my heart says I'm in need of
AND
My spirit whispers I'm deserving of
I make sure not to miss a moment in truth's lessons
BECAUSE
I have trouble trusting I'm deserving
of much more than I have
AND
Even that at times appears as far too much
To give love to you is of the divine
AND
I'm full aware of its depths
BUT
It's this mortal condition-based love I'm yet fearful of
I know one supersedes the other
AND
Can be taught
AND
Offered properly, being as though I'm a current student
I'm well aware
I know not how to trust in another's ability
to be taught and offer
My fear isn't that we don't learn
BUT
Who's understood
I'm preparing in hopes
that when I see you it is evident that you understand

## A Poet Unknown

They don't know me
Really don't feel me
I'm not what or who they think of me
Would probably shun me if they knew
There are days I'm on point with this
and other days I suck at everything
I keep my flaws a secret because rejection is no good for me
But lately / I felt like just being me
Because truth be told the facades aren't really helping me
I am so lonely inside
Even when they are all around I remain
alone
alone
Because no one really knows me
Part their fault and partially mine
for giving my life for all of them
I wake up every day in isolation
My talk / my personality
even my occupation is just
another extension of the fake me
I gotta get away from here/ make things clear again
I've silently burdened myself
with the world's likes and dislikes
concerning my life
I need and want a clean slate
But fear rest at the core of me
Wrapped tight in self-consciousness
It's hoping I'll never break free
I'm tip-toeing around insanity for real
And I'm so made up no one knows just how close I am
to falling over this line of balance

What can I do?
Even finding someone who can answer this
would be a quest
Because no one knows me
And others are so blinded
by the walls of deceit they've built
No one knows me!
No one!
How can this be so?
How have I been living this secluded
for this length of time?
None of my relationships are real
They all carry traces of lies told or withheld
I am in awe even as I write this
Because my "life" isn't mine at all
It's non-existent
I've gotten to good at this / too comfortable with this
I'm not free and it's killing me literally
If I don't get away / start again / I will die this way
Leaving my spirit to hear a eulogy
about a girl I never knew
Setting my eyes on any prize because it keeps me alive
Young but old in spirit
and it just doesn't seem to fit me well
Where to go to find me?
Someone answer me please!
My hope / spirit / and soul
are working overload to keep me composed
And now it's reaching the end
I don't want writings to be all that's left of me
Without ever stepping out of my box and becoming me
I hate that no one understands like me
Hate that when I talk
no one reads between the lines like me

Hate that everyone depends on me
to counsel / teach / and be supportive
I am not the official good girl
I never asked to be
You gave that to me
Expecting too much from me
Well I'm so sorry
I can't wear this mask for you anymore
And I'm no longer a toy for any of you
I need to be free
Because rumor has it
only the best things in life are
I'm praying none of you will hate me
But in the toss-up I began hating me
So I'm flipping the same coin up again
This time if it lands on tails
It symbolizes the end of things in my past
On heads
It means I'm headed for great things in my future
You no longer have a bid in this game
Like it or not I am who I am
The only choice granted to you
is if you will stand by me
Waiting for my true reveal
I've been on my own all along
But for some reason this
seems more alone
Finding me
It even sounds more free
Wanting to get a jump start on my own legacy
Not allowing you to create a mirage of me
So say goodbye to me
This idea of Ashley that you've constructed so well
Hand over the clay it's my turn now

I want to mold who I should become
If life is truly what you make it
Then at this moment
I've made my first attempt at exposing me
Availing myself to life's liberty
I've shared the greatest part of me to the unknown masses
Expecting a work of art to be formed of my words
Trusting I'll be understood on levels only conquered in the hearts of fellow wordsmith
So I'm breathing easy now
Feeling at peace now
Can see clear now
Because at this moment
I'm standing in my own skin now.

## This Journey

I'm taking this journey you see and it's harder than it seems
You know
one of them trips you get excited
and feel real anxious about
Until you get on the road
and you realize
I don't have a map
And this was supposed to be a private trip
a good way to relax
So you don't have anyone to ask for direction
Yeah, that's me right now
LOST
No one to reach out to
and no one to lead me in the right direction
But everyone to rush me / yell at me
and assume I've been on this road before
So why are you going so slow?
Speed it up!
Forced to go their pace
But I'm lost, so I go for the ride
Hoping the ones in front of me
are going where I'm trying to go
because at least I won't be on this never-ending journey
alone
Not taking time to truly realize
that even though we're driving in the same lane
I'm taking this trip / in my car
alone
Should I go left?
Oh no, no I should have made that right back there
I'm just gonna keep going straight

because I don't know where that road leads
LOST
I wish someone would see that I'm lost
and that I don't have a clue where I'm going
But that won't happen
because everybody else is trying to figure out
where to go too
Everybody is going so fast though
They must don't realize that
it's a rest stop we just passed back there
Then we could all stop and figure out where we are headed
Then maybe I could trail you or you trail me
Then at least we would end up at some place
Even if we're lost we wouldn't be
alone
But on this journey ya'll it's every man for himself
Because this is the journey to find self
One that you must take / and it must be taken
alone.

## One Woman

She's compelled / then intrigued
She's stimulated / then fulfilled
She's captivated / caught up/ and hopeful
She's one woman / holding tight
Making every effort not to lose grip
Because you see
this hope she devotes her heart to
It must never falter / it must never wither away
So with her hope gripped tight and her heart open wide
She leaps
She leaps for the little girl
who allows the desires of men to comfort her
Because her daddy never cared to show her
a woman's worth
She leaps for the little girl who equates love with lustful
one night stands
She leaps for the young woman
who struggles to remain sane
while attempting to raise him
And his son
She leaps for the young mom
who refuses to hold her head high
With no degree and barely graduating high school
She leaps for the young mom who
must go without
In order to feed / clothe / and shelter her child
She leaps for the woman who
is hopelessly devoted to him
Because he always says he's sorry as
she attempts to cover the bruises
She leaps for the woman who

consciously sips of alcohols poison
While her mind has been engulfed by marijuana's smoke
Until she can no longer come down from her high
Yet remains lower than when she started
She leaps for little girls / for teens / for young moms
for all women who give their all
And end up empty and waiting to be filled
I am compelled and intrigued
I am stimulated and fulfilled
I am captivated/ caught up/ and hopeful
I am one woman/ holding tight
And today
With my hope gripped tight and my heart open wide
I leap!

# The Abortion

The biggest secret she's been able to keep under wraps
the longest
Heart wounded / pride shattered
and integrity shoved far to the side
Thoughts of what could have been done
What would have been done
if she had only let someone know
what was going on at the time
To embarrassed / too scared
to isolated to be open to the opinions of all others
Lost / confused / and full of self-hatred
She decides to alleviate the pain
the situation she now faces
This life / this being she could never raise right
Take it
Him or her away from me and please do it real quickly
Gone!
She's gone
My little girl
My little girl / who would have been an inspiration
to millions
Through extraordinary creations and heart felt dedication
My little boy
My little boy /who would have been the inventor
of things to come
The leader of billions of lost young men
struggling to survive in paths set by those prior
Without a clue of reality to soon be set free
from the voice of my little boy
My precious piece of life
Given up
Sent away

From selfishness / need of acceptance
And knowledge of my own childish inability to be
or provide the necessary life skills and nurturing spirit
a mother possesses naturally
Or so I thought
Which can't be so
Because I gave up my baby / My first conceived
without a second thought crossing my mind
I deserve to die
I never had the chance to see your eyes
hear your cry for me / or smell the scent of you
A view / sound / and fragrance I now long for
At times become consumed in
Because you are a part of me and I of you
Leaving pieces of myself dead / deceased / forever gone
never to be discovered again for me
Where do I go from here?
Not sure
No answers clear enough or comprehendible
to ease this type of guilt
Inside of me lies a lifelong guilty
One maybe none of you will ever feel
or have the capability of understanding
One that eats at your very soul day and night
Making each day more difficult than its previous parts
Years have since passed
And you still remain a constant
an unshakable / yet unspoken memory
Reality at the soul of me
which speaks to the spirit within me
And freedom is a dream I'll never achieve
without you here with me
But beside me is an extension of you
Mother

A title I've not attained yet
Carelessness still remains a part of me
A child-likeness is still the clay that molds me
at times controls me
Not sure if I'll ever be
Motherly
Obtain the integrity and subtle instincts she carries
I am sorry
What makes this even worst is you can't even hear me
My pleas of desperation
my attempts to make a declaration of peace with you
I am forever indebted to you
My dear
Not even sure what to call you
Never even gave a chance to see if you were a possibility
It seemed so wrong at the time to me
and now my destiny excludes you
Left to jot down my thoughts of you
Or who you could have been
Eyes dry from to many tear filled nights
Thinking the crying would drain me
causing sleep to fall on me
Not have to constantly face this reality
What will they think / say
When they discover
I too am a murderer / A killer of sorts
That evil took reign one day with intent to forever stay
Fed me words to endure as I gave the...
Ok
To suck life from me
Gave a piece of me
Freely
Deceit
I'm still indebted to love I pour

Bought with a price
Now I can spit this Truth
Sacrifice of my first born
So salvations legacy be won
Gives me clarity on days
those days depression from guilt consumes me
When I accept less than a smile
Because in my heart those days / these days
I know I deserve some form of punishment for my crime
But the Divine just tapped my shoulder
so I looked up to question why?
This is what was said in reply
Each burden you've had to bare I've molded in my hands
End result
A creation of my hand
These hands are truth / These hands are love
These hands heal all things
And restores all stripped / torn / and given away
So here under
In these hands / this embrace
I see clouds a little deeper now / smile brighter
at speckles of yellow springing
from the green blades of grass
How sweetness can consume me in just the right wind
When night skies seem to call out to me
I feel beckoned unto the moon.
I LOVE YOU
Don't know you / but feel you
Can't hear you / but know your call still
Can't touch you / but have embraced you a million times
Only God the Divine can vouch for this
But baby / sweet / sweet baby of mine
Mommy loves you!!!

## An Ode to Him My Best Friend

You entered my life unexpectedly
Most felt you isolated me / shunned me
and quickly signed me up to be a member of
The
"Anti-social club"
The
"Over the top analytical club"
The
"I'm just a little too deep for ya'll club"
But what they failed to see / was inside of me
Whenever you'd softly whisper to me
Reaching spaces in the depths of me
spaces I never knew were there
And other places I never wanted to share
Uniting soul to spirit / unleashing a freedom to finally
see me / all of me
Breaking the bans from my hands
and releasing the choke on my throat
No they can't see
The impartation of wisdom you breathe through me
To bring hope to a generation of lost dreams
And courage to those fearful
of soaring higher than the skies
I understand it's difficult to receive
When I tell them how my intimacy with you
causes me to shy away at times
Because you are my heartbeat / my soul mate
my only solidarity
Which makes you/ my first true love
I tell them about being thirteen years old
And the way you would hold me when I came from school
After being teased for
being the "white girl" stuck in a black girl's body

Simply because I enjoyed reading books
and pronouncing my words correctly
I tell them about the lack of self-confidence as a result
The feelings of inferiority to the white kids in school
My desire to see my mother free herself of all others
and just be mine / all mine
If only for a short while
I tell them of your ability to listen
and not interrupt me when I would vent about it
And your hug
I tell them of your hug
You would hold me so tight
In a hug filled with so much love / an unconditional love
The same type of love I would cry on your shoulder over
Because I couldn't understand why it had to be you
and not him
My daddy
Asking you why / why can't I be a daddy's girl?
And very softly you would whisper
of my unique and precious ways
And how special I must be to love one I do not know
yet is the very one who hurts me the most
I tell them how at those moments with you
my heart is revived
And I'm able to move forward in this journey I'm creating
This path of guidance for others to easily follow
Because I love them/ I love them all
I never want them to feel left out
as if they are not a critical part of my existence
So here I am again
Placing all trust in you I confide in you all these thoughts
and as you always have
You softly whisper
expressing the need to continue telling them of you / of us
For in you there is truth / there is hope
For in us there is a voice.

## Tattered Love

When I'm afraid I yell
I yell at you
and I'm sure you can't tell or understand
why it's gotta be this way
Yelling
A sound that made me bound
Placed fear in every cemented step in movements thought
Then abandoned me / isolated me
Present day still making attempts to kill me
you
You equal me
Me without you and I'm nothing
Stop!
What did I say!
Shut your damn mouth!
Stop acting so stupid!
Alright, you gettin' on my last nerve!
Yelling
I'm just afraid
Afraid you will end up tattered just like me / because of me
I just can't let that be
I'm sorry!
When I'm afraid I yell
Yelling again
Work harder!
Don't just let them bully you!
Try harder!
I'm just afraid.
Afraid you too will know of isolations wound
And will endure over twenty years of loneliness
in rooms full of company

Afraid you won't like you
And with all this world has already yelled at you
Mine will solidify / confirm what has become your reality
That you are never going to be enough
But you son / are enough
You have always been enough
I'm just afraid
When I'm afraid I yell
Wrapped in confusions embrace I've tattered our love
I've loved you afraid
Afraid to let you be you
Afraid to see growth in you
Afraid to feel hurt in you
When I'm afraid I yell
So if you measured the times I've yelled
I suppose you are measuring how much I love you
Love you / tattered
Love you / afraid
Yelling again
What the hell are you thinking!
Why wouldn't you just tell me that!
Afraid
When you are afraid / you yell too
Yell from your insides where fire burns deep
and release isn't an option
You're afraid
Afraid to be yelled at again
Afraid your fire will consume me too
We share love / tattered
Remnants of fear's molding built who you've become
I'm sorry I yell
All held in from who I really want to give it to
much like you
You / a reflection of me

We must break free
Which separates you from me
Can't be restored through you
I've placed too big a burden on you
Need these fears to subside / die out / never to return again
Reverse time / take me back to my life's rubble
I'm picking up every piece of my existence
leaving nothing by the wayside
Afraid?
No
Embarrassed
Embarrassed I cuss at my children / ashamed I yell at them
Afraid?
No
Hurt that you left me / again
Ashamed I'm now like all the rest
simply a baby mom and not a wife
Afraid?
No
Insulted that my character wasn't enough for all of you
Ashamed I come out of myself in an attempt to fit in
Afraid?
No
Confused as to why my body and mind
never seem to add up
Ashamed I gave away
what only my husband and I should share
Afraid?
No
Devastated you thought it was appropriate
to steal my precious piece of childhood
Ashamed I repressed it until it was too late to tell anyone
Afraid?
No

Too self-conscious to see the true beauty within me
Ashamed I missed out on connections as a result
Afraid?
No
Depressed that me needing you just wasn't enough
Ashamed to call you dad
Afraid?
No
Hungry for your attention
Ashamed I never understood you core's view
Afraid?
No
Silenced in a great big world / I'm ashamed here
Here my innocence is once again found
I open my hands and surrender these ashiz to her
to you
Finally / I'm free!
Whole and complete
Son / this is called transparency
no longer a tattered vision of love
Transparency allows us both to see love's true remedy.

## She's Come Undone

Everyone has that freedom inside
locked away deep so you'll never find
That freedom you try but just can't justify the way you feel
Its two sides to you it's true
but the freedom that's inside of you
To huge to push away
Away the urge to just release and be who you will be
Ahhh... This magical feeling / this joy I'm feeling
It's good for me/ it's so good for me.
FREEDOM!
It entertains me and always relates to me
I just can't shake it / it's urging me to let it out
But I'm scared it's much/ too much pressure for me
Can't sleep / I'm feeding on it
Wish to straight get lost in this
Too good to be revealed in its finest state
Ohhh... This escape who dare to debate
I love who she's becoming
Love how she's looking now / how she's talking now
Best of all / what she's thinking now
Thoughts she never thought possible
filled up with so much bliss not allowed to let it out
But it's calling me / it indulges me
Needing me to just oblige it in this task / this journey
I call unity with the natural and spiritual worlds
What can I say in adornment at a feeling
This utopic finding
that somehow makes so much sense to me
And I bet it would do the same for you
if we all were free enough to let it out
Only breathing / only alive when bits of you are released
You are the very rhythm of my beat
With each sway of my hips

giving away the fragrance of your liberty
Whenever it seems you're fading out
through this guise of life
You reappear greater than before
leaving me in the most lustful state one can imagine
You pleasure me!
You arouse me!
You send me to heights never surfaced before
hit depths to deep to translate into words
At times feeling so surreal to this whole idea
Must remain connected to you
You keep me composed
just thinking of how good it will be the next time we meet
So please / don't take so much time to come back to me
I've waited so long to find you / approach you
Now embracing you like nothing I've ever known before
I moan passionate purrs of seduction in your presence
You and I are meant to be one
much more than a form of chemistry
This here is destiny
manifesting itself in the more exotic tone
My world away from this world
My escape route and haven when things get to tight
You make everything alright for me
You literally turn darkness into days
Days where sunshine comes from my insides
and expose futuristic views of you and me
We are what's left for the world to see
Now come to me / and taste a sip of harmony
Let me give to you what nothing on Earth can buy you
no amount of luck could grant you.
Now close your eyes with me
and visualize life's finest views
Mmmm... Intoxicating you are to me
I'm all loosened up / my soul is free
for once I can let my guard down and just be / me

I wish to drown in this
somehow learning of elevated dimensions in you
In order to somehow grow closer to you
become more of a part of you
Through your lens I see realms yet to be mentioned
ever spoken of
I want to be re-grounded in you
creating some grade 'A' foundation
Deposit into me the answers of life to come
I desire to be impregnated by you
Impart your glorious philosophies into me
the open vessel for you to be revamped through
Store your legacy in me
I will surely die like this / but I'm always alive with this
I'm realizing you are too big to fit on my paper
As my thoughts of you continue to protrude my mind
my hand won't write fast enough
To little ink to fill my pen
penmanship not neat enough to attempt to describe
What a fool I must be to try and confine you
I must set you free!
Allow you to exist in the imaginings of minds
who only dream of having you all figured out
There are too many levels of you
and although I may never see them all
I need to exist in you
Thinking of ways / ideas
of how to make an adequate description of you
How to explain your whispers in the air of all who inhale
Yet and still I sit here / pen in hand
Persistent on having ink droppings
spell words in your favor
Hoping all who hear me
have the chance to experience a moment / in you.

## It's Calling Me

You can't tell me I'm not destined to be here
sharing my voice with the masses
You see / this is my grenade / my weapon
my poetic fight for the generations
So / I don't look like you / don't sound like you
don't act like you
News flash!
No one can fill my shoes so I choose / rather refuse to
become another you or you
Because that would lead / to less of me received
In the lives of those who depend on me
to be the voice of reality
My true identity caught up with me
Causing me to face the real me / the good / bad
and especially the ugly
So in this journey of becoming me
accepting and loving me
I've conquered new heights locked in my memory
of a little black girl with dreams to reach her destiny
Unleashing sacred phases in me
that exist throughout eternity
Thoughts racing and continually chasing images of a
renewed mentality
One where minds are open to receive the beauty in truth
each time spirit and soul join
Giving birth to a nation only the heart can conceive
I am the invention / created by the master
to breed the next generation of immaculate seeds
The oil / to fill empty vessels sucked dry
I am a mother's kiss / that mends their wounds
The well consumed / flashy / and so renewed

The burdened / lost / and sorrow filled
The pleased / relieved / and overachieved
The pleaser / user / and abuser
The mothers and daughters with hearts of scorn
The fathers and sons confused by masculine absence
The lonely seekers dying
in the universal attempt to be comforted
accepted / and loved
So for all you'll who still doubt / let me say it again
I was destined to be here / born to do this
Couldn't exist without this / wouldn't be free without this.

## Carpe Diem

Seize the moment
Each moment
So you won't have to go back in your mind
and rewind time
To conjure those memories you left behind
Words left unsaid / others simply watered down
Illusion of what's really pounding at hearts beat
That 1$^{st}$ / 5$^{th}$ / or 7$^{th}$ kiss and you still somewhere stuck
wandering in clouds' fog
Pretending to be lost in the stars / when really
As soon as lips part / your mind also parts
Into space / the space between reality and memory
Where you play back / moment on repeat
How it could be / should be
Consider what you just missed / let slip
Moment went to quick
Promises to self that next time you'll fully embrace
Take moment and let it soak in
Feel warmth of lips before they've even touched
gravity's yearn as two become one
Hands placement / grip or caress
Meaning of tongues stroke / soft and slow
And just like that
the words can no longer be watered down
This captured moment
Leaves no word unsaid and the depths of these words are
finally understood
Creating more than a memory
because in a moment seized / we've connected to eternity
Experienced the truth in carpe diems' existence
For when children grow / and blossom they will

Far off and wide as the fields in which they once played
All innocence unguarded
two feet they shall independently stand
One mind in regards / and it's in sole control now to decide
Those car piles of junk / juice spills and temper tantrums
soon regurgitate
As thoughts you'd like to rewind / then bottle in time
Capture lap sized bodies to cuddle again
in toddler framed bed
Pause
Now/ place small fingers in between yours
search each scar
Feel now its story / its pain
real or attention hungry / feed it anyhow
Hear behind and inside cries
now / discover each teardrop's message
Answer now / to the call of nature's lead investigator
Seize the hunt
parenthood unknown but what treasures to be found
Just don't be so quick in letting the journey pass you by
Seize this moment here
Attentive crowd / your voice
Pause
This moment / seize here
My voice / my life on display
Purpose given to me / this is artistry
Write words to carry crowds wherever I choose
Hear numbers they're willing to pay
just for five minutes of my time / yes / my time
This is precious time
Our moments / moments in time to be seized
So I feel the dryness
and cramps of belly before arriving to the venue
Swallow more frequent

down throat that surprisingly remains dry
Release sweet
Power packed adrenaline / forms as my name is called
my name
Seize that name
A name labored for
Count steps to mic / mindful numbers too have definition
Stand
Pause
Here / this moment
Inhale these eyes on me
spirit breathes
So before I ever speak
we all have taken existence in eternity
Carpe diem
For this moment has been seized.

## Persistent

Here I am
Still standing
Stronger than I ever was before
no doubting my legacy anymore
Truth came through / snatched me up
sat me up in the highest of realms
Told me it had a few stories to tell
So here I am / yeah it's me
Take another look / ya'll stuck now
Never thought I'd make it this far
bets on me never busting out that box
But my / oh my / how the tables have turned
Speaking my mind / divulging the divine
giving no never mind about how you feeling this time
Pushing pause / in order to create less noise
Allow my voice to echo through winds that soar
Because here I am
Still standing / stronger than I ever was before
From this height/ past is too far beneath me
Present/ rests beside me as I'm nestled at futures' throne
Time / no limit
Realms / no limit
You really thought you stood a chance
Thought four walls / four corners
your tall tales and bottomless pit had did me in
But here I am
I reversed the spell
Turned your wicked into gold / your lies to sweet honey
Your darts to purpose / wherever they may land
I told you / I'm limitless
So here I am

The place you never thought I'd be
The same place that's never really been far from me
you just masked it so I couldn't see
Now / I'm so far up I've escaped your view's limit
So anytime I spit words like this
I simply step down to remind you of your place
A step stool
The powers never been in your hands
A tool used as the true master was grooming me
Step by step molding this master piece that is me
And here I am.

## My Light

Sometimes it seems my life was made of
sorrow
chaos
confusion
Anything that brings a heart to misery
A dream to be what this world needs
A son to mold into a man / no daddy to mention
Things in my past / too much to recollect
Can't begin to reflect because / life goes on
Or at least that's what they say
When their piece of the pie was
so much more sweet and good to eat
So / don't look back
Just keep hope alive!
Strive for the best!
Winners never quit and quitters never win!
Like somehow those quotes
close the gates / bars
no more like concrete walls
That were built in those tear filled nights all alone
Yes alone!
But all the fear / hurt / heartache and pain
must have come out on this particular night
In each drop that fell on my pillow because
when I woke the next morning I saw a light shining
And no / I can't say it was the sun
and it wasn't that bright idea either
I mean/ I wish I could say this was my idea
A light bulb that went off in my brain
but this wasn't me at all
There was more to this light
than my mind could even grasp at the time

I mean this light seemed so complex to me
because it was shining every time I closed my eyes
But when they opened / Gone / just like that
Unbeknownst to me / this light would guide me
This light would mentor me
This light would lead me to you and you and you
So today / at this time
Through my heart / soul / and mind
through the words that I can no longer keep confined
I present to you / that light
This light in me that your eyes can't see
it's given me the very ability to capture time
Inspire minds
and circumcise hearts to be taken up in my rapture
This light / was given to cast a glow
on all that seemed dark / barren / and bound by walls
It's so simple you see
an internal cleanse and take a look at me
That light has been set free
now able to shine ever so brightly
The light inside me has become so clear in my memory
This light is mine
one only my eyes can see
but makes up the me that you all can see
Words
Words are that light that dwells within me
Given to me as a gift / my gift to share with all of you
to share with the world
Words
A series of speech sound
that symbolizes and communicates a meaning
Words
Used to express your hearts feelings
Words
Do my words really carry weight in the universe?

Because I remember hearing the old folks say
Sticks and stones may break your bones but
Words
Words will never hurt you
True or false?
True or false?
It use to wonder / I would really ponder
But it must be false / it has to be false
Because
Words
Words are all I have
Words have made me who I am
Words are the rays of sunshine that brighten all my days
So you see
Words
Carry more than weight / they carry power
And I've made proof of this truth
this fact at this moment
because my light is shining bright
And without any of you expecting / my light
Brought in the form of
Words
Has captivated each mind hearing or reading these words
Words
Words are my light/ that light shines through me
We all have a light that shines within
We know it exists
yet sometimes fail to acknowledge its' brightness
It took me 22 years to acknowledge my light
So I declare to all who hear my voice / or read my
Words
Let your light be made known to everyone / in every way
everywhere you go
You'll be amazed how bright you glow!

## Internal Evolution

Ashamed of her testimony / but who said she had to
She says ashes and dust are what's left
she feels boarded with guilt's stares
Because remnants of past sins keep her locked in / boxed in
She sees no escape route
No friends around so there's no one around to pull her out
comfort her/ then push her out
But even there she's scared
Outside that nice little shell
that one little space that fits just right
So snug in a place whose grips so tight
it sucks out the very life
She's literally dying to live
Caught up in a dream that's become her lie / her secret lie
her lullaby
Her ruins / she's justified them / nurtured them
Clenched tight to the vice
that's sifting her every breath away
Times two never meant a thing to her
because round one was simply the norm for her
Dysfunction overruns dismay
and sorrow out runs subjection
And although they're running / she never saw them coming
Believing in a dream that was built on lies
she sings her goodbyes
Forced out of the very lives her womanhood birthed
Destitute she sits
Tears fill empty palms because there's nothing left
She already gave her best
the best good in her/ the best bad in her / all of her
Now gone from her

because she deposited in this world of hers
Now out of that world into one so unfamiliar
so opinionated / so unforgiving
A world that won't reveal to you that there's a third world
Because it's in competition with that world
what world / whose world
Can you imagine?
She was just banished from her world
So confusion sets in
standing stagnant in the midst of contrasting worlds
She spots a face / a very familiar face
So she reaches out to touch it / to see if it's / a real face
And as she stretches farther for it
it begins to gravitate towards her
Force field between three worlds begins to form
As her foundation begins to crumble
her footing has been shattered beneath her
She knows she must move fast / jump fast / react fast
And into the grasp of a familiar hand
with a familiar touch / gently guides her into its' world
With fear mixed hope
she looks up to see that same familiar face
She begins to weep / she weeps looking into a face
that looks like hers
Smiles like hers / accepts like her / desires like her
forgives like hers / and loves like hers
Yet she's not even sure how to receive this view
Doesn't know how to bask in the warmth
of these serene cradled arms
Perplexed with the similarity she sees
Can't cope / because it's her face she sees.

## Life's Awakening

I've been reborn
God's assurance in reassuring me that all has not been lost
That each dream shown / every vision unfolded
is a guarantee
The Divine's promises to me / lays me down
adorns my body in calm
only lavenders' essence can contain
Crowns my head with playful daisies halo woven together
and stares at me
Remnants of past sins gone from me / cleansed from me
Presented me back to life / pure once more
So here I am
"Tha Rebirth" from Ash'iz where my beauty began
Same place where I learned truth's definition again
Where loves' transparency divulged details
that intellect could never explain
So now I feel with more than simple hands
Taste with more than simple tongue
I hear through more than simple ears
Smell from more than simple nose
and have sight of more than simple eyes
Yes! Tha Rebirthing of life
has become my awakening to life's' honest delicacy's
With my hand grazing along yours / we embrace
Pause
A moment
Soak up / destiny
Here
Connection / your spirit to mine / touch aligns
I've encountered the Divine
With tongues tremendous ability

to decipher flavors diversity
I'm left without longing
Here / destiny
Soak up / this moment
Pause
What sounds abound
now that joys symphony can be heard
Inhales consumed of sweetness
caught in blossoms of sun rays
And rainbows promise
is seen illuminating the moons glow
I now embrace
Pause
This moment / each moment
Soak up / it's destiny
Here / my entirety in connection with eternity's calling
Each piece of me composing wisdoms vibration
echoed throughout the existence of all mankind
It is here / I unwind / have come undone
Epitome of what my origin calls home
Such a sweet resting place / Here
Destiny / I soak up every moment
Pause
I finally have realized all I am inside
My declaration to life / is my life
Nothing taken for granted / I welcome it all openly
to ensure its understanding / to levitate on its truth
only to be lifted into sky's vast unknown
just to be tried again
Elevation in rebirthings core bares new life
into my origins intimate legacy
allowing me access into all that divinity sees.

# I Am

I am not alone
Not forgotten / lost / or misused
I am not today's example of how to lose
the choice every refuses to choose
No not I
I am not ones door mat
not the weight hanging from your coat tail
the subject of your disgust
No not I
For I am
Sensitivity's confidant
Sweetness squeezed from honey / laughter's life supply
humility birthed / and love prophesied
I am not a body / not a big butt and breasts
not hips and lips / not your fantasy's bliss
No not I
I am not weak / not less than / not equal to
not kin to this world / this generation
No not I
For I am
Infinite wisdom exposed / beauty's mold and maker
The natural mother of nature
and the journey one takes for hope to be found
I am
Amazing / just glance at my creation
I am
Serenity / as my palms unfold feel peace revolve
I am
Happiness / transferable it is
simply lose yourself in these brown eyes of mine
I am

**Legacy** / I never die / never grow old / I / must live on
Evolution of this universe
is in my control
I am
**E**levation / ascending to heights incomparable
unimaginable
I am
**Y**outh / in a futuristic view
I mirror the mystery in youth/ the innocence in youth
the core of youth
I am truth
I am divine
I am one of a kind
I am ASHLEY
**A**mazing **S**erenity **H**appiness **L**egacy **E**levation **Y**outh
I am poetry's mission
Carpe diem's origin
Loves sweet spot
The intersection of intimacy and sensuality
Wisdom's revelation / and God's creation
I am me.

## My Poem to Self

She unto me / I unto her
So in honor / today I will embrace her
Me / We / Yes / something similar to the trinity
My mother / nature
making me this natural nurturer of all things
Today I embrace gentle winds
blown of butterfly wing echoes / kind of heart in me
Embrace the strong tower / root solid in ground
oak standing tall / spine of me
Yes / natural nurturer in me
Embrace hands small / as seeds planted deep
This touch blooms of humanity
reach your core/ and conjures all you will live for
Venture they dare / to the depths of me
Embrace my attempts to ensure none drown
embrace ability of transparency to cleanse them
Yes / me / womb of alchemy
Concocts fragrance you long
never intend to become consumed in
How dare you
My mother / nature
life's care taker and I / life giver
Yes / me
Embrace the silent sounds inside breaths air
heir to spirits throne
Sitting high in order to embrace it all
Each vibration / hearts beat
rhythm echoes and creates profound sound
Embrace tears formed in the wells of me
To my virginity / I'm sorry
Yes / me

Today I embrace me
Muddy creek your water became
So many sturdy appearing
weak levy / wood rotted kind of men
And Me
In tune to this river's flow / flowed
Today I embrace forgiving me
Yes / me
Similar to the trinity
Mother / nature / me
The sacrifice revived of loves spirit
Forgiving me
Two beings alive of me / one still abides in me
Yes / me
Once a murderer to life attempting to escape me
Embrace my sorrows
Gray clouds simply part because / you sunshine
Remain hidden in clouds / where rainfall kind of tears
weep from heaven's skies
Today I embrace / me
Autumn leaves falling kind of brown
Caught up in my mother's rapture
time enough not to touch ground / withered dead
Yet close enough to know dead / and embrace her winds
refreshing of being born again
Yes / me
"Tha Rebirth" of all things plain but beautiful
Pure / but lived
Funny / but pained
Innocent / but wise
Transparent / but scared
Loved / but alone
Eternal / but carnal
Sensitive / but courageous

Yes / me
Unto her / she unto me
So I honor
Today I will embrace her / me / we
Yes / something similar to the trinity
My mother / nature
making me this natural nurturer of all things
Including / embracing me.

## The Glory of My Story

You can't tell my story
Can't revive what's left of my story
You just wouldn't survive / my story
This broken place / renders such a lonely space
where heartache and its' antics
have become the beginning and the end of each chapter
You see / flipping pages use to be my minds way of escape
Shattered attempts to read upon pages afresh
Imagine new words in order to create a better reality
As not to usher myself
into the sly embrace of defeats arms
But / when you're born into sorrows essence
distortions appear as clarity's kin
Making truth in beauty and destiny
much more difficult to depict
Resulting in arms weakened
now too tired to turn one page
Fingers tight / wrists paralyzed / exhaustion sets in
All fight for life gone from me/
and you stuck staring at me / steady judging me
But see / you can't tell my story
Can't revive / what's left of my story
You / just wouldn't survive my story
So weak / worn / and tattered
The pages of my existence growing slim
because with each day that passes by
They steady blowing off
into the gusts of wind that engulf me
Swallow me whole
then toss back fragments
of an already bruised heart and mind

But with these withered / stained shredding before me
Coupled in surrendered palms
births fragility's peak
Transparency consumes me
And each piece is gathered
and displays a more brilliant chapter than before
So I continue to read more
As truth beckons me / strength is restored unto me
Making these pages less heavy to hold
in what once were feeble hands
Where wisdoms wealth now secretes
offering words to now write my authentic story
Now I / can tell my story
Have revived what's left / of my story
I survived / so you / could tell your story.

## I Wanted to Write a Me Poem

All I wanted to do was write a me poem
Since the start of my writing feelings down
I've tried my very best to convey exactly what I feel inside
Mainly inside my mind because
I've learned that's my easy escape / the momentary escape
And it's just not enough / it just won't cut it
So / I've decided / no determined
to clearly share my heart
I mean the depths of me / where I'm offering the world
Well / hold up
Possibly just the few of you gathered here listening to me
But / the world sounds so much more befitting to me
Yes / I sometimes / well / most times
get carried away in the words I say
But anyway
giving all of you
the opportunity to see all of me
To love me / or hate me / and honestly
it scares the shit out of me
Literally / the shit out of me
And yes / I need to know what I'm saying makes sense
Although I'm rarely concise and repeat the same things
more than twice
In extended versions from its previous parts so the listener
can understand
Even if they say they understood the first time
Quite like all former lines in this "me" poem
I'm trying to scribe
So yes / this scares the shit out of me
The bloated fear filled gas
that keeps all my courage in a constipated state

So although its painful / and quite the shitty process
Once released / I'm left with nothing
but the best in me
Able to give ya'll / the authentic me
You see / I've been wanting to write a me poem
But every time I pick up my pen
I jot some thoughts down that usually transform
into some form of love poem
You see / love poems come real easy to me
Because although I've never truly experienced it
how I write it
I trust if I make it clear enough
next time it comes my way I can comprehend
Receive / and let love have its way
No guards / no resistance
no false god
pretending to be appointed to my royal legacy
Just love / trust / vulnerable
Me / him / kingdom come
My heart restored
more like enlightened / elevated
Because giving / has always come naturally to me
See / love takes my hands away from me
Replaces hands / for wings
grown from shoulders with blades
Debts paid / burdens bore
So within moments notice
I am strong enough to carry wings so bold and grand
To be raptured inside them / inside myself
Me / for serenity
True love/ now exposed/ wings open wide / ready
Soar along sky
Painting hues of hidden messages for my king to decode
on his pilgrimage to come find me

Stroke of each cloud to engulf his dreams
with memories of me
Here / in this / my most transparent
highest awakened place
So when he awakes
and the subtle moon has given way to sun's rays
He will remember his smile when he first met me
And the warmth will usher his soul back to my bosom
Because within the cradle of these wings / these arms
is home / resting space / his origin place
So / do excuse me / now I'm back
back to the origin of this poem
Me / who you can see wasn't lying about love
It truly will captivate me / and leaving others to become
infatuated with me
Or at least the value of experiencing
all that comes from me
See if I'm going to write a "me" poem
I can't go on without making note of that fact
because I feel it's become my own trend
And you know folks love the latest fashion trend / they do
So they wear my love
in adornment of its silky / rich feel to the touch
until it becomes last year's accessory
So they keep me tucked away for safe keeping
Because we all know fashion trends
simply repeat themselves
So no doubt they know I'll come in handy one day
just not today
But for the sake of this "me" poem
I'll protest this indignant use of my loves infinite abilities
In an attempt to protect my sanity's limits
Because writing comes so much easier
to a warrior of my kind

All action / no voice
Letters on a sign never seen
because I'm too afraid to raise it high
All the while knowing
my throats release of words unspoken
conjures skies reply to the divine
Which I've found
has always been where my depth resides
You see / I wanted to write a "me" poem
A poem to somehow let ya'll inside my insides
The sacred layers that make up the grace and mercy of me
The darkened tar in me / stagnancy
Needing another's movement
to entangle this spiral that is me
Become silver lining through the core of me
Stretching all the way to my crowns access
on the other side of my chemistry
Tell me now / can you feel me?
Outside the bounds of articulate wording
and matters molding that in the end/ won't matter
Can you see me now?
Possibly understand the more goofy I am
the deeper you've dug into my golds mine
So would you be mine?
Could you be mine?
Won't you be my neighbor?
I know what you're thinking / no she didn't / but yes I did
Just brought Mr. Rogers back / and while I'm at it
I can't go on without mentioning Barney
you remember / the big friendly purple dinosaur
The one I wished all my child hood was my neighbor
On my block / 321 Sesame St.
With the homies Bert and Snufulofogus
Because they understood

an introverted / extrovert of a girl that was/ and is me
Yes / going on tangents is me
See all I wanted to do was / write a "me" poem
But with so many random thoughts protruding my mind
I stopped to engage in meditation
Attempts to align these chakras of mine
in an attempt not to overwhelm ya'll
And although the feeling so sublime
Coming back to life on this side
leaves / me void of a stimulation
only found in solitudes love line
So I rise / only to try and intellectualize
all that just occurred during reflection time
So I ended up with this / and if I don't stop now I'll be talking for days
Because I haven't figured out how to arrest the flow
of knowledge that circulates through
"my" mind
Because even when I'm giving it my very best try
Wisdom comes alive / and instructs me never to go blind
Yes / 3rd eye comin' at you
And while I'm going there / let me just add
conspiracy theories aren't conspiracies really
Just truth
the masses can't wrap a finite thought pattern around
So it's labeled the evil foolishness of the world
And I'm not just saying that because I'm a believer
although I am a believer
Besta believa / queen diva
Just because I heard it on a t.v. show
And my mind thinks it needs to flow
in rhythm or sync to what I'm saying / or possibly not
I just wanted to throw that line in this poem somewhere
you know it is

A "me" poem
And if your lost at this point
and not sure what on Earth I'm talking about
No worries / go check it out
Because isn't that how we all learn / doing the research
Research the corners of my mind
have you not for the past 7 / 8 / 9 minutes of your time
You've been waiting on my "me" poem / haven't you?
So here goes
Good evening / I'm Ash'iz
Ash'iz "Tha Rebirth"
Well / now that I think about it
This poem sounds a lot like "me"
So please / feel / absolutely free
to read between the lines of "me"
Discover the abyss / that is Me.

## Me

My smile is of the sun... my heart of the moon.
My smile is of the sun
Brightens all days / all day
Delivers warmth when cold
draws heat in order to usher you into its' living waters
Yes / from this son water flows
all while illuminating the globe
My heart is of the moon
Glows the night sky
Offers light to all in its' darkest state
Illuminates the beauty that's within
Causes all to adapt at its' arrival and reign of creation
Yes
My smile is of the sun... My heart of the moon
And you are now infused with the essence of all things new

www.ingramcontent.com/pod-product-compliance
Lightning Source LLC
Chambersburg PA
CBHW051703040426
42446CB00009B/1282